BE A PINEAPPLE STAND TALL WEAR A CROWN AND BE SWEET ON THE INSIDE

NOTEBOOK

This Notebook Belongs To:

Habit Tracker

Start Date:

Habit/Goal	1	2	3	4	5	6	7	8	9	10	11	12	13	14	15	16	17	18	19	20	21	22	23	24	25

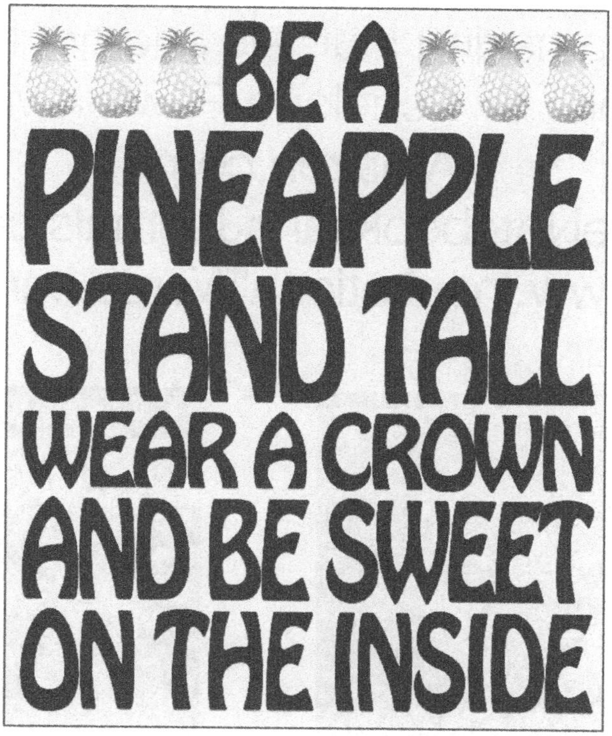
BE A
PINEAPPLE
STAND TALL
WEAR A CROWN
AND BE SWEET
ON THE INSIDE

Support comes in many forms (purchases, likes, and especially Amazon reviews). We truly appreciate all the support our patrons have provided us. As a "Thank You" for your continuing support and as a token of our appreciation, below is an QR Code for you to download a **free** "Be A Pineapple" 8x10 printable PDF*:

** For Personal Use Only*

For more amazing journals and adult coloring books by Penelope Pewter, visit:

Amazon.com

CuteNotebooksandJournals.com

www.InspirationalWares.com

She Believed She Could
So She Did
Adult Coloring Book with
Inspirational Quotes
A Coloring Book for Grown-Ups Providing Relaxation
and Encouragement for Women

She Believed She Could
So She Did Adult Coloring Book
with Inspirational Quotes

The
BE A PINEAPPLE
STAND TALL,
WEAR A CROWN,
& BE SWEET
ON THE INSIDE
Adult Coloring Book

The Be A Pineapple
Adult Coloring Book

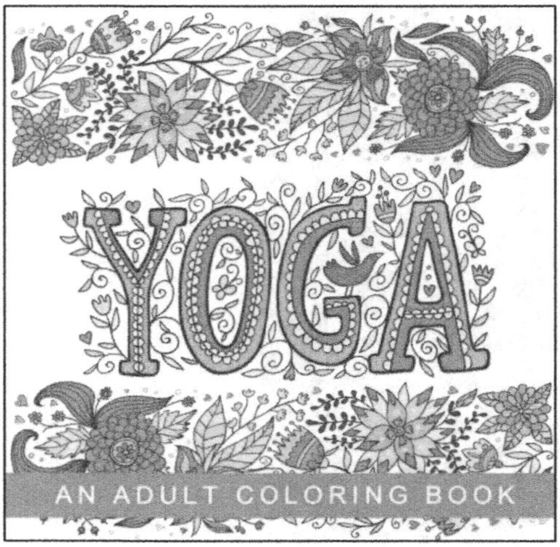
YOGA
AN ADULT COLORING BOOK

YOGA
An Adult Coloring Book

The Adult Coloring
Book for
Coffee Lovers
A Meditation and
Stress Relief Coloring
Book for Grown-Ups

The Adult Coloring Book
for Coffee Lovers

Made in the USA
Monee, IL
19 June 2021

71781343R00063